Uncomfortability

Roxanna Bennett

Edited by Shane Neilson
Cover and interior design by Jeremy Luke Hill
Proofread by Sheri Doyle
Typeset in Linux Libertine
Printed on Mohawk Via Felt
Printed and bound by Arkay Design & Print

LIBRARY AND ARCHIVES CANADA CATALOGUING IN PUBLICATION

Title: Uncomfortability / Roxanna Bennett.
Names: Bennett, Roxanna, 1971- author.
Description: Poems.
Identifiers: Canadiana (print) 20230441319 | Canadiana (ebook) 20230441327 |
    ISBN 9781774221020 (softcover) | ISBN 9781774221037 (PDF) |
    ISBN 9781774221044 (EPUB)
Subjects: LCGFT: Poetry.
Classification: LCC PS8603.E55955 U53 2023 | DDC C811/.6—dc23

Gordon Hill Press gratefully acknowledges the support of the Canada Council for the Arts, the Ontario Arts Council, and the Ontario Book Publishing Tax Credit.

Gordon Hill Press respectfully acknowledges the ancestral homelands of the Attawandaron, Anishinaabe, Haudenosaunee, and Métis Peoples, and recognizes that we are situated on Treaty 3 territory, the traditional territory of Mississaugas of the Credit First Nation.

Gordon Hill Press also recognizes and supports the diverse persons who make up its community, regardless of race, age, culture, ability, ethnicity, nationality, gender identity and expression, sexual orientation, marital status, religious affiliation, and socioeconomic status.

Gordon Hill Press
130 Dublin Street North
Guelph, Ontario, Canada
N1H 4N4
www.gordonhillpress.com

May you be free of suffering.

contextual field notes & grateful acknowledgments

As an interdependent being I acknowledge the earth, water, fire, air & aether of which we are all composed, the cardinal directions, the trees & plant beings without whom we would not exist, our animal siblings on & under land, in ocean & air, the moon, the stars, the sun. Boundless gratitude to the generations of Indigenous people who have stewarded this land since beginningless time.

These poems were written during 2020 & 2021 in response to the pandemic as able-bodied sane people were given more financial support from the government for a temporary illness than most disabled people receive for lifetime disabilities, while the rhetoric around vaccines & social recovery failed to include those who have never been able to participate in our culture's idea of 'normal.'

As a disabled person who has been housebound & isolated off & on for most of my life, lockdowns & quarantines didn't change my daily life much except that I am now able to grocery shop for myself & family (thank you, Instacart).

Versions of some of these poems were written in correspondence with other poets: Khashayar Mohammadi & K.S.Y. Varnam. Others were written inside of online workshops with Hoa Nguyen exploring the works of Bob Kaufman, Lorine Niedecker & James Schuyler. Other poems were nurtured in Turtle Disco Zoomshells, online workshops with Stephanie Heit & Petra Kuppers.

But most importantly, these poems were written through daily meditation & yoga (thank you Adriene Mishler) beneath a maple tree, while feeding my friends the squirrels, raccoons, blue jays, grackles & sparrows.

The poem "Certain is Untrue" originally appeared in *the way out is the way in: an anthology of disabled poets*, edited by Stuart Ian McKay, League of Canadian Poets chapbook series, 2020.

"Gendermental" appeared on Zoeglossia.com, a Community for Poets with Disabilities.

The poem "The Fall Bundle" borrows lines from the work of MLA Chernoff, Kevin Heslop & Aaron Schneider.

I first encountered the word "unenabled" in an essay by Khairani Barokka in the anthology *Stairs and Whispers: D/deaf and Disabled Poets Write Back*, edited by Sandra Alland, Khairani Barokka & Daniel Sluman, Nine Arches Press, 2017.

Medicine Baskets, Body Bags refers to an exhibit by Indigenous artist Bonnie Devine.

Kapala is Sanskrit for "skull" & can also mean "a drinking vessel made of a human skull." *Kapalabhati,* also called "breath of fire" is a pranayama or yogic breathing technique.

Sangha is a Sanskrit word meaning "community" often of a spiritual association.

Tonglen is Tibetan for "sending & receiving" & is a meditation practice to cultivate a sense of equality & compassion by exchanging self for others.

Thank you to the generosity of the Ontario Arts Council & the Canada Council for the Arts.

Endless gratitude to guardian angels Jeremy Luke Hill & Shane Neilson.

Love to Kirby at knife | fork | book for tirelessly making pretty spaces for poetry & for being the last person to visit me in person in 2018.

Love & solidarity always to Dominik Parisien.

Thank you to Síle Englert for hydra-time & the line "I'm out of spoons, now all I've got left are knives" that I stole for the poem "Our Lady of the Flies" & for the image of the Fonz on a surfboard in the poem "The Prime Directive".

Thank you to my karma chum Kevin Heslop. Thank you Papa Heslop for the laptop. Thank you Joey Saltarelli for your generosity. Thank you Kyle Stark for blue lotus tea. Thank you Shirley Jelliman for all of the gardening wisdom. Thank you always to my buddy, Steve Jelliman for letting me steal lyrics, & my offspring Connor Bennett for being.

Table of Contents

spring: our nature is to die

summer: we will meet again soon, if not in these bodies

fall: feed the fire your uncarved head

winter: hang me with oranges, let the birds eat sunshine from my skin

... & spring: Do What Thou Wilt shall be the whole of the law

spring:
our nature is to die

We were so close, there was no room / We bled inside each other's wounds / We all had caught the same disease. — Melanie, "Lay Down (Candles in the Rain)"

Revel in the Ruin

In April the animals arrived in
crypts of ice, thawed-out old diseases
skipping species. In summer we discovered
we're all in this together, parading
first responders through unpeopled
streets. By autumn we've forgotten,
locked-in our bored & our wanting, gunned
each other down for TP & belief.
Free us, our cloven-footed Majesty,
O Pan, moving through what's left of the trees,
now we have all been unenabled, unfree,
now we are all worlds to ourselves, each other,
lovers, revel in the ruin because in winter
we'll remember our nature is to die.

All Quiet on Every Front

In winter we remember our nature
is to die & salt the Earth with our denial.
Lie with me awhile. The future keeps failing
to arrive. Cells multiply, divide, splinter
into timelines when we set aside our pride.
Be small with me under the dirt, take no
pleasure in causing hurt. Tunnel inward
together for warmth, in thrall to all quiet.
Tomorrow's for tyrants who force us to
count, *one is for sorrow, more is for mirth,*
heaven is plenty for everybody.
Wealth is our birthright: sweetgrass, sycamores,
stalactites. Crow takes flight. Into the endless,
made spacious by the unpeopled places.

Certain is Untrue

Now we are hollowed out, made spacious by
the empty places a pixelated
world created, now Themyscira is
surveilled by Google Earth satellites
& people-shaped topiaries replace us,
now Metropolis is a wilderness
& the "widening gyre" is quietly
re-seized by the birds of prey,
now craving certain & untrue, we stage
drive-by birthday parties, sidewalk bagpipe
serenades, now that Amazon isn't
a river & fires ceaselessly rage,
no one's coming to our rescue but each
other, same as another, wreathed in light.

Life Without Weather

Free us, O Pan, from our temporary
madness: cities, "sanity," sameness,
distracted by delusions of difference,
release us from this dreamed poverty
of indifference, cursing out-of-stock
masks while warehoused elders die behind locks.
Now we are all unenabled, unable
to act, now we have all had a sample
of feeling the lack, now we have all lived
life without weather, backed into corners
by forces much stronger, by doctors or
coroners, now that we are all disabled
could we begin to love each other's pain?
No one needs to fight. We are all the same.

Prisons or Prisms

Now that we are all disabled, welcome, friend,
here's your table, we've been expecting you.
Take a seat & we'll unveil the truth:
it's normal to be sick, unjobbed, unfun,
it's normal to resist what's advertised,
to sing the certain song that we all die,
that's all we're certain of. Our era is
not forever or even very long,
a fever song out of season, one we'll
forget later, resealing the quiet
glimmer of cleaner air. Robins
belly flop April's chilly daffodils &
windows are prisons. Or prisms. We hide
ourselves from ourselves in every season.

The Unwinding Empire

I am the dream of the unwinding
empire & its schemes, the laughingstock of
the afterlife for the absinthe-minded.
In the harlequin forest turtles talk
turkey, dinosauring rudely for
daffadowndillies. I plant stargazer
lilies & can't stand   working   but a garden
turns keys   in the dirt, it won't hurt   anymore,
organ harvesters, whoops, I mean doctors
mock orange snowbelles wilting while the clocks
starve us of hours. Hospitals/holding pens,
compassion ends when institutionalized
"care" begins. Admit we don't care, people
die, we think it's fine. We could change our minds.

Keepers, Cousins, Angels, Reapers

I am the Night Mare, meet me in Albion
by moonlight, bring your diary but leave
behind the iron fires. My children
of the night, such music we will make of
the unwinding divine. The body speaks
the mind into meataform, a formal
diagnosis speaks for & silences
us. Sit & stay, "Golden sunshine all along
the way." As waves of crowds evaporate,
who was I without them anyway? Strangers
are my keepers, cousins, angels, reapers,
everyone, everything must fade away
& reform in other Clayface flips a
Roman coin & the empire ends its day.

"You Can't Spell Unclean Without Uncle"

Goodbye gambling, pay-per-view, we'll be
fine but if it's our time, go gracefully,
quit hoarding TP. I still don't know
what NASCAR was for. Why do we treat our
selves like debris, unholy? Most of life
is unpleasant physical things, settle
in, Uncle Nature's going to touch you, make
you sick, molest you, then kill you when he's through.
{Assassin bugs adorn themselves with bodies
of the dead, each spoon-shaped back is unique}
I love my pervert drunkle & his handsy
tuck-in tickles, *You can't spell unclean without*
uncle. Thank you for eating our shit, flies,
someone's got to clean the rot of empire.

Let's Get Weird & Hairy

Let us stay then, you & I, far from the
gaze of the all-seeing eye. For I have
felt the dismissal of the omniscient
physician & resolve to keep inside.
Machine Gun Mary's getting weird &
hairy while micro-dosing LSD. Kermit was
right, kids, it's not easy being green. On
screen our ghosts grow hungry for the nameless
secret country on the real's periphery.
Play with me. There's infinitely more than
we can see. Meet me at moonrise with
Clayface in the ruins, dance on vaseline
with me. & the parliament of owls
will make our income guaranteed.

Are You Experienced, Have You Ever Been

The hippies were right about everything,
kids: recycling, LSD, trees, peace.
Remember when we wanted to be free?
Not brands or branded by "community,"
iron-clad identities as though self
is fixed or a commodity & a bodymind's
worth can be measured in money. Easy
for me to say when the OAC pays
for my poetry. I feel guilty &
grateful & needy & hate all attempts
to pin me to a fixed state of being.
Steve interrupts to bring me my prescriptions.
I'm sorry, was I spinning conspiracies?
Wake up, kids, they're all true, please believe me.

The Unknowing

"Lifeproof" the new floorboards declare, as though
there is a charm to ward off storms. Do I
dare, do I care, that to eat a peach leaves me
too weak to be "normal," to rake or mow
or shovel, but I can crawl & slap on
stain in cat-cow to cover pressed pine planks,
drag a rag dripping with Home Depot
chemicals across the deck's expanse & fake
the colour of dead wood. Death is the white
cat hunting the dark-eyed juncos & the whitecoats
shunting patient caseloads, sending people like
me home to die. Alone. The unknowing
hate sick, think it's a problem, want it gone.
Like golden dandelions on the lawn.

Unweedable Garden

But I believe grass is a weed & try
my best to relieve it of being
a blade in a monochrome uniform lawn.
I sing the bodymind electrified,
driven inside by the empire's long con.
Night bloomers are shy but their perfume emits
with soft insistence the fragrance of home
grown strangest in the shade, my skullgarden,
"Nonsense, plenty of flowers blossom in the dark,"
said Shirley when I was churlish about 'prettiness'
dying under burgundy maple leaves. I try my best
but I was born weak so I must go slow,
sow patient seeds & swallow my screams when
I'm sawn in half by painstorms without relief.

Unbearable Burden of Being

Each day I calculate my liver's long
odds against acetaminophen & diphenhydramine
& brace myself for eventual organ & other failures.
It's the little things: barometric pressure's
the sharp tip of an icepick ground down
to merely fatal & I panic at the piano wire
slicing through my cheeks & the ever-shifting
suckhole that used to be my teeth & try
to breathe into the space where my face
used to be, faint signals from fingers, feet
fading away & I'm frightened, so much
less I can do every day. Slow death from
taking painkillers one at a time or
a quicker kill, all at once. Kinder.

"The Angel of the Marriage of Contraries"

Am I possessed? Prove this is not a haunting,
a curse, what's the difference, electricity,
spirits, I'm sorry for being "crazy,"
pain is maddening, generating
the same thoughts again & again, grooving
patterns in my head: am I pain's parent
or its offspring, its supplicant or victim,
is it my teacher, am I hallucinating,
making it up for attention, it can't
hurt this much without killing me, what does
it want from me, I've already given
it my first-born child. Demons or neurons,
chemicals or sorcery, all alike.
Helpless on the altar of authority.

Skin Starvation

Now Steve's home ALL. THE. TIME. & so's my kid,
no wall is thick enough & I'm too thin,
again, unwilling to dislocate limbs
when there's no one to reassemble them.
What's it like to fuck & feel fine, to touch
& be touched & have a good time? You think
you know skin hunger, raindrops are *too much*,
try lying beside a lover you can't
love, on fire with want, for days, weeks, months, years
& years of nothing much. Choose to adjust,
to resemble memory means now's not
enough, how much more do we need? I fear
my need but need to bear my fear, befriend
my hunger, anger, greed. Learn to accept.

(Un)relatedly

I believed I was alone but our bodies
need other bodies to be, their labour
& care & exhaled air. Grocery store clerks
keep us fed because we forgot to break
bread with our neighbours & seem to believe
food comes from freezers, property is real,
poor another species, sick can't happen
to me...I'm sorry, a squirrel is grooming
their tail, fluffy! I'm training my attention
to soothe sensation & the sentient
beings all around me, earwigs, redwings,
maple trees. Is it greedy to want to
be happy or the most selfless generosity?
I love you no matter what you believe.

Uncle Nature Loves His Urchins

The maligned masculine old pervert hangs
high the prayer flags for the unwinding
empire, piles high the old rags on the clean
pyre. My star, some flowers are born old, some
seeds don't grow. We know so little & less
as we go. Can we outgrow? The good
elm holds the full moon, mulberry branches
wound round the suet cage confound the cagiest
squirrels. All-colour tree, you are red or
green or not depending on the downy
headed woodpecker, scarlet cardinals,
Solomon's seal pale blossoms in filtered
gloom. "You can't kill a Hosta, not even
by trying," but will I be able to garden?

The Pontifex Institute Prepares Your Pineal Gland for Viral Upload

People of suburbia, quit fighting
the lawn, monoculture's wrong
for the planet, it's gone on far too long,
this denial of the weather, our senses,
our nature is to die would be an awfully
big adventure, said Pan to Hook. Wendy
warms up leftovers for her lost soldiers
& tucks them into bed before picking
up her book. Keep passing the open
windows, the universe is a pinprick,
an iris, a shinbone; a sunk ship is
a punch card for martyrs far from home.
Diamond, dove, delphinium, I am one
of a million Nephilim descendants.

"The Trees Are Never Tall Enough, It's Never Enough & It's All We've Got"

The ideal form is shapeless colourless
tasteless odourless sightless legless
handless headless genderless Shall I be
tender Shelley to your Byron or are
we bored of the same old wine ink dark sea?
Dear Diary, I am the Night Mare, meet me
in Albion by moonlight, leave behind
the counting houses, iron fires. Between
Scylla & Charybdis: Tartarus
where sleeps our Mother of Monsters with glossy
sailor pearls for eyes. O please let me eat
your body born without the unfortunate
luxury of sensitivity, hench for me.
Be my blood & tongue to speak for the trees.

Dark Shadows

Who among us is blameless but everyone
unknowing of the suffering they cause.
It's cost effective to cut off the infected
member, cast off our other, all shadows
are Darkwing Duck runs under the fence again
proving April fatal to the over
eager for spring moves in its own sweet time
is an illusion, lunchtime doubly so
since gastroparesis took its toll free
numbers can't define trees, me, anything
really, more exists than we can perceive,
love, hunger, misery. Now flowering
peace from history, our grief a garden
feeds billions if we put the us in them.

Skip the Dishes with Gastroparesis

You wish: you still have to wash the blender,
order protein powder, reishi powder,
just add water, clean the spoons. You live in
terror of tubes. Takeout's more essential
than funerals in this same as the old
world. I miss fucking & food, double
doubles & stockings, insensible shoes,
hooks & buttons, stupid shit like stubble
burn from kissing, I'm no Mary Poppins,
having somewhere to go, knowing who played
who in that show, checking in because
someone wants, wanted, to know, how it is,
I miss spanakopita, copping a
feel, how do you cope with imminent death?

summer:

we will meet again soon,
if not in these bodies

O preacher man / Shoot me with your poison arrow / But I dance on Vaseline.
— David Byrne, "Dance on Vaseline"

of Moss & Mycelium

Monday is a menstrual cramp of the whole
body, Tuesday's loose tooth, fucked fingers on
both hands, Wednesday's unhumped, Thursday thirsts for
an untwisted throat, fuck right off Friday,

reminder of all undone, Saturday's
unsated, unslaked, sat out on sidelines,
Sunday spins-out, covets missed boats. Neighbour's
pandemic pool parties are louder than

poetry; I wanted to write about
moss & mycelium but Steve needs to .
tell me about his new boss & my kid
just found videos of giant spiders

that eat entire possums. No matter
how you try, "You can't indict the cosmos."

Gendermental

She shuffled on buckled feet unsteadily
down unlit streets, She was incurably romantic
but unfuckably delicate, who was She
anyway but semantics, shorthand

for a surging field designated bodymind,
ego/I, the implication that a word means me.
So strange, any word, divination by name
is dropping more anchors onto this plane

I want out of, but into the pain is the only
way through, we're all Mad here & the wait time's
cruel. This week's diagnosis is next week's
detox dilemma, the Dalai Lama

talks of thankfulness, long-term bliss, not this
quick fix when I micro-hit cannabis.

Dreaming of Babylon

I don't speak the language of medicine
but I still have a body, I don't read
the testaments of churches, I know I am
holy, I don't buy the stories they sell

you, they seem like baloney, you can't get
cancelled if you don't subscribe. Is the really
real world   outside   in the quack shack, mallards
ask for crushed nuts unfisted from feminist hands,

emerald-headed, iridescent, the missus
caught a pretty one this season & keeps him
dreaming of babbling on & on for no reason
is more than opinion, has no substance,

as a weapon, harmless, if my mind is spacious
enough for the outrageous.   It's a practice.   Takes ages.

Our AI Babies Welcome Future Alien Archivists

My kid pries up patio stones to make
shrines for animals, subluxing their bones
as they go. Omens of coronal shift,
the noosphere is an ocean for phones.

I hope our AI babies hone the craft
their parents lacked to make the Earth their home,
greet alien archaeologists with
loving kindness when they come to pick our

bones. No one is free of suffering until
every being is & no one is alone.
Why fight the lawn, dandelions spill
golden wine, no one wants to work this hard

or needs to, it's fine to let the flowers
bloom & die. Summer's too brief for murder.

I Am the Autocrat

Hannibal, set the table, dinner for one
& seven billion undone by a viral infection
of separation, the cold delusion,
no one means more than another one.

In the hierarchy of pain I am
the autocrat (am I a loser?). There
is no game. "Medicine Basket, Body
Bags" mother cradled, man-made graves, I gave

in at the office, lost the book, forgot
to save. What's essential isn't profitable
until you're miserable. "This is my design,"
Will says to climb inside the mind of a fellow

human being, those who hurt us are in
pain, it's worth remembering again again again.

A Canadian National Exhibition of the Bodymind

"I feel there is a devil in me," I said,
misquoting Ferlinghetti misquoting Cocteau,
"continually mocking my better angels."
When they fired me from the Crown & Anchor

because I couldn't use the microphone,
I stole pocketsful of silver dollars
to squander on John Player Special &
nachos; paramedics threatened to cut

the leather jacket from my passed-out body
as if my problems could be solved by eating
broccoli & other privileges I can only lately
afford. Ford is tortured by delusions of normal.

All I ever wanted was   not this
anatomy   like a stretched-out   stocking.

Unsung Song of the Bard Owl

Giddyup psychonauts, the pox unlocks
our auric architects. Unboxed: the hidden
alphabets coughed up. Humble gifts, barred owl
on the back fence slow blinks, unrepentant.

Opportunity's noxious, a knocked-up
ninth grader from Oshawa unmasks
the worst of us. Thousands of elders dying
in trash: future us. It hurts, it hurts, laws

don't work or no one would be behind bar
hopping or breathing masks. There must be
other options. I lost my pop-up shelter
in an online auction & can't speak much.

Parade Her round the monuments dressed up,
a token of the unspoken song gagged shut.

"Apples for Algernon"

the vendor cries but no one is buying
gene-modded fruit from abusive lions.
A dollar digs another diamond mine
but the daffodils arrive to speak their mind,

we have to listen now it's time, there is
no time. *This is the mission, quiet down & listen*
to the singing in, the inward vision
of a planet with no isms or missives,

no missiles or directives, no need for protection
when everyone is undefended, slip off
shallow pretence, assume the position.
Corpse pose a challenge for the gallows-minded.

They hung Her from a gibbet in an iron collar
after nine long months in the hospital tower.

Automatic Stigmata

Bring me your suffering, bleed out your poisons,
the goddess of misery serves billions
daily. Give me your tender anger &
terrible mercy, defile me. Nothing's

sacred when everything is holy. Worship
me (at a distance, theoretically),
give up the delusion of separation
& safety, we're all sick until we're free.

In the garden we harden lupin,
delphinium, with a thin-edged sickle,
pardon the daffodils for drooping, are we
through demanding flowers form as function

to logic's conclusion? Nothing ends
an argument like a letter of intent.

The Devil's Business

When they fired me from *The Computer
Paper*, I still don't know what I did but
I remember the terror, how to feed
my kid. When they fired me from

the gallery because I couldn't cut
a straight line (but kept the director
who molested me & was arrested for
drunk driving), I put away my sketchbook

& haven't touched it since. Amphetamines
to get to work on time, Wellbutrin to
fit in. We hurt ourselves to make a living
but is that living, then? Or living death.

There must be more than this. Baby-buying
on the dark web, wet markets. Old business.

Unfund the Almighty Charlatan

Let's realign good with common, reconcile
with resurgence, it's urgent. Grandmothers,
please teach us to feed ourselves peace.
Who knew food grew on trees? We were

conditioned to idolize ignorance,
fashion worlds from stolen materials
for its jealous god. The almighty charlatan
flings down his angel wings, straps on

his gatling gun & gives in to fan demands
& chimerical manufacturing plans.
No one needs a spray tan but Apocryphon
codices could come in handy because

some conspiracy theories are true,
they have lied. But so have you.

The Sheeple Look Up, Always Up

No one is not changeable, to whom do
I belong   sun-charged   It is not August, yet,
sunrise that never heals. We will meet again
soon, if not in these bodies, bloodflowers

under a new moon. Make room, make room
for the sheeple looking up at the doomsday
clock while the wise sow seeds in the Earth's soft
dark, pride is a sin I was taught so I

tried all my life not to parade that I
loved & desired & trash-talked everyone,
even you, even Hoa. The world is too
much up my ass, in my pocket, in my

ears, in my closet & why are there Disney
stickers on this bunch of bananas?

Unconditionally Yours

For a thousand dreamless nights skinned on the
moon's teeth, hungerwrithe, your rubybruised body
mine. Gnarled dragontoe divine, need me like
a demon saturnine. Yesterday I

was alive in golden sun, tonight I am
ice. If it's forbidden, I love the hidden
things like the organs singing under
the floorboards. I'm never bored

with dramaturgy, it's all a stage if we're observant,
time & its materials will serve us, I am
unconditionally your servant.
If hyssop is a mirror for kestrels

over water, the moon forgets her argument
with the Gemini temple's daughter.

Mourn Her Descending

Rue river.   I was a wing-bone urging
verse in waves for home, dancing ground solemnities,
graves   unless   how much less   am I than those
that endow us with long-stemmed blue roses

Do not save ruin   the all are   I possess
at the organ hunger for wonder, born
in swamp, sworn through the mouth in ugliness, now
the oak leaf to be sold. Turn away torn,

what is freedom to grief   I am a reed.
{Through this we circle her face, the place of
surface tension}   A hummingbird rises
sinks, mourns her descending. She who knew ropes

dandelion greens   marigolds   duckweed
secret ways to wade through newly dead psalms.

Unfazed by Strangeness

Refrain refrain, the dead need no cages
& the living need no stages. "Give us
a statement, declare, aver or be negated."
Weightless friendless but also object less

is more than we expect not to get get get.
We fear wildness I was taught but loved
the animals who fought back, bit & scratched.
They never act. I wish I could tell lies

from fact but faces shift in certain light
& weather & who am I to say or
judge another? No one but an awkward
gawker at the altar of the Mother

of us all guns its furry wings, gathers
speed & springs, singing, into the dark.

It Won't Always Be Like This

But of course I love flowers & wax rhapsodic
for hours on the drowsy towers of foxglove
nodding off. I forgot the beautiful
is unbought. Thyme creeps green

between stems of delphinium reaching
for the sun needs us to shine on, is love.
Collaborate with wise bodies, access
summer, archive winter, respectfully,

Grandmother, how will we weather the weather?
Recollect being a woman situated
at the stake, sacred basic emanations
cleared the room of easy certain girlhood.

It won't always be like this, piratical
devotions to tolling the people bell.

fall:

feed the fire your uncarved head

As a species, we should never underestimate our low tolerance for discomfort.
— Pema Chödrön

The Fall Bundle

You go. I stay inside, waiting. & did
we lose our strangeness, did we live with our

sordid diaper squelches, surplus of Mad
eline crumbs, Ensure can pyramids? Did

we prefer to jerk off to jazzercise,
manifest west our animatronic

spectacular? Did we mind sanitized
static, six feet between group coffins &

panic? Were we couched, all too often
forlorn, our wants uncrystallized? Were we

whispering triptychs to the aether in
porny exclusion? My CPTSD

deprives me of, it's nothing serious,
life, I was floorbound before the virus.

Ungrateful U-Turn

I look forward to Western medicine
catching up with ancient wisdom,

to be treated like a sentient being,
not a specimen, a future organ

donation, an inconvenient aberration.
Normatives grope at "normal" like pervert

drunkles at a funeral or maybe
I'm ungrateful for the way fate plays its

artfully loose hand. Divergent from the current,
taking evolution's U-turn with it,

they say I'm sick, sick, sick, because I won't
can't not stop mimicking the pricks & their concepts

of illness & wellness, that every bodymind's
the same while coffers & coffins swell like a virus.

Dear Diary,

I have nothing to confide except this
secret: at every moment, in any

moment, I am telling myself: "Don't start
screaming" & trying not to cry. Today

I screamed & am ashamed of letting out
the built-up pain. To resist: suicidal

ideation, despair, hate (self or others),
advertising, the thick-skinned pharmaceutical

war machine. To return: Uniqlo socks
(7% wool), spring, dignity. To

reschedule: movement disorder specialist,
therapy, transitions, streetcars, stairs, scents,

strangers. To regret: not knowing the last time
I danced was the last time I danced.

Do Manticores Dream of Basilisk Teeth?

Dance around the question: who benefits
from elections, prisons, schools? Compliance

with a system makes us tyrants, makes us
tools. There is no way to sit that doesn't

hurt, purple my legs, leave them numb, but
I can't leave the writing undone. Cling like

a suckered barnacle to the anchor
of poems as canticles, knackered past

reckoning, what can I bring to the crowded
table five minutes from tube-fed:

disruption, narcomancy, some cheek.
Do manticores dream of basilisk teeth?

The heart-shaped prism dangling from
fishing line in the kitchen angles for peace.

Dance on Vaseline

I can't trust doctors who mean well but still
believe what they can't perceive is unreal,

I mean, no one can see hunger but we
all know how it feels. Sickness is normal

& "normal" is a concept & concepts
make us sick. "If you're well enough to dance,

you're well enough to punch in, interact."
I can't act, make transactions & the fact

is none of this is a choice but the consequence:
crumbs snatched back. Calculate the damages

from countless inquisitions: What colour
is your pain, what rainbow is your language,

what flavour is your mind, what label makes
a life worth less than theirs or hers or mine?

Unprincipled Certainty

Did my doctor molest me when he tested
to see how far I stretch before snapping?

Saturn is lovely this time of the year,
the outer rings dazzling. When he slipped

the sharp tip of a pointed stick between
my legs & lips, was it necessary?

Did the surgeons abuse me when they
slit me open, took my organs, left me

unable to walk or eat? Why did they?
No need for them to cut me. When they

gave me Fluoxetine but told me it
was a stomach remedy, gaslighting?

Who is the authority, them or me?
They hurt me eternally with certainty.

Mutually Assured Resurrection

Steve varnishes the dollhouse floor I fucked
up with my rubbish fingers. Today is

harder on my mother wherever she
might be. Mutually assured destruction

or resurrection? Happy unbirthday
to me. Thanks for the insight to skip CA's

workshop, if their somatic rituals
worked maybe they wouldn't panic

about murdering the Earth. What if
the punishment for matricide is the

virus? Traffic sluices rain up over
its tires like it's urgent to get some

where else. & I'll slide this notebook between
its siblings back on the Ikea shelf.

The Subtle Crucifixion of the Chronically Dystonic

What the fuck is rent? We'd rather kill or
die than let in strangers to not suffer

in winter. We shame our ancestors &
descendants, never mind our elder

dependents, future us, going out as
we came in, bald, shitting ourselves, needing

to be spoon-fed. We are all interdependent
but even among poets I don't understand,

this isn't performance but you want me
to stand, I can't stand, give a hand, this is

all that I am. Not on sale, not a brand,
can't pretend being able to withstand.

I don't need more fucking technology.
I need worth measured in love not money.

Of Bloom & Fallow

Anger is the weather, an energy
like any other, it comes & goes but grows

without release, a creeping skein. Some days
I can't say if my pain is "really" rage,

a Buddhist therapist once told me there's
no difference. I used grant money on

an acupuncturist who said emotions
live in our organs, imbalance in one

affects the rest, which makes sense,
we are all interdependent. There is

no fixed self but try telling that to the
government. Shifting into different

shapes & states is natural. Hello trees
& your cycles, seasons of bloom & fallow.

Feed the Fire Your Uncarved Head

November petrified, essential as
a morning sky, evenings among amber

keep free Bury future dinners lacquered
green   Not to consume   storm's epicentre

in stone   Forget all you ever knew, in
visible irradiating, seizing

She came in like a starving deer   boards &
sawdust, sleepily as an unwatered

plant on which sits   Feed the fire your uncarved
head   asleep   thin & bricked   one who goes barefoot

barehoofed in snow   Drilled into dots & dashes
pebbles in a pocket parts of town oddlit

up close   Chimney nests turn lungs into winter
wings   shedding glass feathers when they go

Wild Strawberries

Mary Shelley, your creature is my child
foraging wild strawberries, tomorrow

they dine out. Not I. Li Po ran after
gods & goblins. Blake, angels. Me: I am

an unclean reed. At the window, another
revolution, turn of the wheel. A pall

lingers in my body, your noose my roller
skate cracked off your skull. Cute kid, crown

of plastic bobbles on your head, are you a
blackbird now or someone else's little

unloved sib? Deep fall, run away home &
how Unabomber were you, brother?

Impossible to be alone, everyone
is a person: bugs bigots racists ghosts.

Witchhammers

Now that the grackles are gone what becomes
of us. Now the elders have died warehoused,

who comforts us? Remember outside? How
we tried & tried, what connected withered

us. What if disease is all in the doctor's
head, what if proof is more than specialists,

diagnoses or scans? November can't
decide how to sacrifice its children

& what divides us but winter, secrets
of the beehive, witchhammers. Scrape a rake

against the morning before the ache sets
in & these hands can't say what they mean.

To live   is a gift & prismatic   or
a prison in this thin skin, impatient.

Pinprick, Iris, Shinbone, Sunk Ship

I know, the days are endless, eternal
& the nights, vertiginous as you shrink,

the universe is working out its kinks,
& we call it cancer, lupus, covid.

Somewhere, a woman shaves her hair, enters
a frigid cavern for the next twelve years,

elsewhere a grizzlyboy prepares to chant
for his *sangha*. Time collapses in

a fucked-finger snap, prophecy passed on
before breakfast, I wake up Mad deep in

my closet & begin every morning
with Buddhist bullshit. The universe is

pinprick, iris, shinbone, sunk ship. Grackles
ask: *Can we pass beyond language unlimited?*

Wood of the God Corpse,

clawing out the hand to screen page or glide
gently greyscale from the quiet   "I like

small frightened things, humans & other meaty
beings"   Into the unspeakable holy

twilight falls   an   artificiality
to worship   the body   & the baleful

blue vincapervinca   crawls   or a
phoenix may fly   into the circle,

a garland on the way to the gallows
Project pale puppets at the windows

closed to negotiations, tactics (the former
starlet in the attic) Antics of feint & attack

sick   what does it mean   to be   allowing
old leaves to slowly fall, dissolve into new growth

Autumnal Every Thing

Why catalogue cut logs? Fall is melancholy
the continuity of which you are

a violet turbulence, cloud clotted
Halloween borrows time from the enflamed

trees, the woods lit   milkweed pods light clear water
colourless   its surface exposed   stumps of

deadening the appearance of   Beauty
broken by the ice   woodashes snowbearing

sky smeared with weak armatures   pale tender
French blue, an odd place lightly flattened with

the richness of use   Piled-up junk, one tin
window shuttered chickened thistles The shuddering

winter will be levelled for our viewing
pleasure by complicated machines

winter:

hang me with oranges,
let the birds eat sunshine
from my skin

I have always depended on the kindness of strangers. — Blanche Dubois

The Organ's Expression as Emblems

"It's just a word," Steve said when he heard but
            later a word that couldn't be said, a word
that spread, like tentacles, the doctor said.
            Why put that in a patient's head, subcon

sciously they want us (them) dead, less trouble,
            it's inevitable, ill health is inbred.
Or are we bred to keep the empire fed?
            I don't accept (I radically accept) that

we can't prevent, please don't let the doctors
            deal more death, they prefer it to inconvenience.
Billions of minds prismatic, infinite as trees
            in billions of beautiful bodies the colour of meat.

We could play together like the monkeys we are,
            tarsiers, orangutans, chimpanzees.

Untouchable

Death is the white cat hunting the dark-eyed
            juncos, whitecoats carving crystals from your
throat. You will sing the unwritten note. They try
            to be so helpful, shunting patient caseloads.

The walk (or my crawl) to the operating
            table means overriding instinct,
all animals wisely bolt at a blade
            but we are Pavlovian, salivate

to obey. I don't speak the language of
            hospitals, do I still have a body
or have they stolen & dissected it
            for further study. Your soft throat barely

covered by a paper thin bandage, *un*
            touchable cancer-crusted carotid

Never Let Me Go

When I met you outside the dog museum
          I was my own ghost, with a heart full of
hummingbirds & a black apple lodged in
          the throat. For seven years no ceremony

resurrected me. It's subtle, the alchemy
          of transmutating trash to gold, nothing stays
the same old. Grow ancient with me, like rain
          & stone & wind & flame & hold me but

let me go, never let me go. The only boys I knew
          who liked poetry only loved their own &
the girls, even worse. & who needs the competition
          for each other's inattention. Nazaré

was so cold the wind cut my skin, what doesn't.
          Hold me, Buddy, when the world rushes in.

Meet Me Outside the Dog Museum

Let's run away together, Buddy, just
          you & me, meet me outside the dog museum
at a quarter past threeve, you are maple
          tree & I want to be a weeping willow

but I'm destroying angels, the fungus
          under all of us, occurring simultaneously,
you in a snowstorm in the Malhavoc
          van in Madison, Wisconsin, me cheating

on what's-their-name with their cousin, non-stop
          flights of fancy. Grow old with me, a thousand
years or more at least, too much I haven't
          been or seen, teach me to eat the black apple

down to the core & plant cyanide seeds
          coronal lantern auroral. Don't leave me, please.

How to Give a Sponge Bath With Broken Fingers

Medicine as bureaucracy is a
        system of irresponsibility,
if there are other paths through the dark forest
        they won't be found inside the hospital's

proving grounds. Am I able to witness
        this process in presence, am I able
to give sponge baths, meal plan, with these fucked hands.
        Rot is inherent, like oil in sesame,

the full moon fulfills cyanide in
        apple seeds, you are radiant irradiated,
sunburned inside your throat. I want, I want
        & suffer. What can't be bought: your heartbeat

beneath my cheek. Please, don't go, I'm so weak
        I can't speak. How many times can I die in one week.

Please Send Help

Artificially milked to silence years,
        days, to enjoy loathing a smile. Cripples
huddle for outside   what weather   is months
        years inside without   Winter wrings us out

ragged   sleepless   formless   a flattening
        of the senses.   Traffic as ceaseless as
heartbeats heart beasts but   inessential. I
        am not suicidal. I do this, I

do that, the chasm sings, the mirror beckons.
        I do keep opening the door the sky
reckons.   I do not free the dragon   I
        do sleep on the floor   I do not   believe

in isms. I do dream of the hidden
        machines but I do not   eat   the prism

Snowability

Damply electric, desiring   Pain
        like this in which a small flock of ink-dipped
birds unlove a secret city. Pinkening
        snowfields at sunset, untinted roses,

shrunken bluejays   unbelievable   petroleum
        byproducts   Above these thoughts   spacious slow
other   not thoughts   January disgorged
        the year's impersonal tears in thirty

day chunks, more or less. The lessons:
        definite February, hard blue. Colourless
tarpaulins iced over. These short days endless
        in a pattern   grind muscular   surges

ashore   naked, tarnished   Hang me with
        oranges, let the birds eat sunshine from my skin

The Pause as Neptune's Possible

Ganymede   dawn rose   a golden eagle
        & a grey-haired red-garmented hag   She
who holds the bloody trident   eats the foods
        reserved for the dead, gives by mother-right

Lambspring   the forest, the body   In Winter
        the Old Sow, the fool's finger a full udder
of seven stars holding seven   white poplars
        for the coffin cradle   kneels at the mouth

of the baetcylic mother goddess,
        allows heart lotus to shelter the fuchsia hind,
the scapegoat sacrificed to anti-domestic
        dreaming   The shrunken breasts of the hag are

war in heaven,   the cosmocrator,   the red egg
        which she ate   swallowing   three violet   lapwings

Seasonally Unaffected

I tore out my scientific heart, fed
        it to the wolf cubs & the Zephyr, what
is the littleness of men to the North
        Wind? Ask me the scale of my pain & I

gift you the red eye of Jupiter's storm,
        unblinking, eternal. "Lady Ice, did
you know the world was lonely too?" Bundle
        up, buttercup, & get outside, drink in

the cold clear winter light. The sun didn't
        set when November left. You crept inside,
rejected the freshening bright, green plants
        still tender, upright, the infinite sky.

Yes, the cold has bite. But so do I. Make
        peace with the seasons, the real reasons why.

Chain of Commandments

Taking shelter in a box fort in winter
        I feel like a kid, dependent on Steve
& the government's largesse, but other
        times I feel like a tyrant assigning

tasks to my kid: "Give Patchy these peanuts,
        take this spider outside so Steve doesn't
kill it, I mean if you can, if you feel
        up to it." Thank you Justin for the hand-

delivered legal weed, our community
        mailbox is unshuffably far from home,
I miss the postal worker who knew my
        name, said hello. Whose big shot idea

was is to make February longer?
        Solitude makes us stranger, hacks off hope.

Love & Peace

When the weather isn't their favourite,
        some people are able to go away
& avoid the sad jizz of geese in
        February. Winter is relative,

dependent, "If nothing was OK, no
        one would do it." Our nature is to die
but we salt the Earth with our denial.
        Water remembers oceans are rivers

are channels are runnels etching faultlines
        in firmaments, nothing, not even
the internet is permanent & I'm
        too tired to be my neighbour's police.

They're the same as me: sentient beings
        suffering in pain, wanting love & peace.

On the Interconnectedness of All Things

Joey the Foul-Mouthed Botanist teaches
        my kid the Latin names for what sleeps beneath
February, dormant Persephone,
        squirrelsicles skittering over thin snow.

Pack the vape pen with the good shit, fetch
        the Made in China Mexican blanket
from Amazon, HeatTech from Japan.
        Am I a drug addict if each time I

want to die I take a hit? My kid passes
        the micro hitter with the Pink Kush
from Kamloops as I slather peanut butter
        on the empty suet cage, rationing

bird seed. The endangered woodpecker
        hasn't heard about our quarantine.

Tonglen in February

Green sprouts from outgrown skin sloughed off, flowing
                into forms free from concepts of common.
You are uncommonly formed & resist
                being shoehorned. I breathe in your breakdown

& breathe out bluebirds, I breathe in your fear
                & breathe out wonder, inhale your anger,
exhale long summers. Inhale your wounds
                & give out Bactine, Band-Aids, benzodiazepines,

blankets, books, bad movies, black tourmaline,
                in the drama & out the cool-down. February
is just a word to dread when it's plus six.
                I fed the whipping doves what was left, bereft.

Not everyone can be normal, none of us are Sappho
                but we all know how to burn.

Theory of Relativity

We don't know who we are, could be, without
           rupture, war, divorce, cancer. Regular
is relative & particularly
           fond of red-winged blackbirds. Starlings return,

I sow the yard with microwave popcorn,
           Wasa crisps spread with sunflower butter,
beet chips. Out of peanuts, now no one will
           visit. Steve KT tapes my thigh back in

place & purees sweet peas & squash for the eight
           hundredth day in a row, why cry, any
day now, rows of blossoms, violet heartsease.
           I wish it got easier. Remind me

why I do this, please. (Am I a loser?
           There is no game.) Will winter ever go away?

... & spring:

Do What Thou Wilt shall be the whole of the law

Nothing exists; even if something exists, nothing can be known about it; and even if something can be known about it, knowledge about it can't be communicated to others. Even if it can be communicated, it cannot be understood. — Gorgias 'The Nihilist', *On Non-Existence*

That Was Hell

I wasn't comfortable with crowds, blacking
out in lineups, I wasn't comfortable

with loud sounds & group sign-ups. I wasn't
comfortable being made to wait to share

my pain with strangers, wasn't comfortable
with doctors who put my life in danger

for professional pride. "Why are you crying"
& other uncomfortable questions with

stranger answers, "It can't hurt that bad,
you must be lying." I wasn't comfortable

with poverty, hurting my bodymind
for money, being separated from

my kid when they needed me. That's what we
do, culturally. I tried.   I changed my mind.

Failing the Course in Miracles

If we wanted to cure cancer, we'd keep
Steve & his mother in a lab under lock

& key. But miracles don't make or cost
money, it's not profitable for oncologists

to work toward their own redundancy.
Forget what you've been taught, the wars you've fought,

& give in. None are guilty, none have sinned,
no need to forgive. All are dirt & then—

What if Gorgias the Nihilist wasn't,
we misunderstand. Philosophy is

Gormenghast. Nothing exists, not even
cancer, language has no answers, we can't

understand what we can't understand. Can
we hang out here, inside the ampersand?

Angel's Egg

Love me, love the weight of the ampersand,
the impermanent pause & affective

egregious, Gorgias the Nihilist
nailed it, the paradoloxogia,

to communicate impossibility
is impossible to communicate:

angelic eggs laid by gossamer ghosts,
abandoned fountains spurting bandaged hands.

I give up hating the rats & roaches,
the transphobes & conservative voters,

the cops & doctors, surgeons, social workers.
I am as much you as the family

lamp & the lion & the lamb lies down
on Broadway, on Bathurst, on Albion.

Sympathy for the Bedeviled

I am not uncommon or rare, I am
everywhere. I've seen me in waiting rooms,

subways, streets, onscreen, behind the mic
reading poetry. I am legion, in need

of lotus tea & sympathy. Cast me out,
throw away your own strangeness &

sensitivity. What luxury, to
do what you like pain-free, to move & feed

yourself without injury. I've never
been contagious but treated like, it's out

rageous but rage ages, separates us,
is outdated. Help me, please. We're the same.

Please don't leave. Don't fake it or try to make
me do the same for you for one more day.

Our Lady of the Flies

I dug out my own eyes with a runcible
spoon, now I'm left with just knives. Surprise

surprise! A seven-headed hydra springs
to life. Raze your tablets, children, stolen

the garden, forlorn. Who there wandering,
cluster grapevines hanging, goldfinch timid

singing, groves lindens, aspens (all one tree
being), (months go by & nothing). Scotoma

scintillating or a portal opening,
sick of spinning, groping for handholds &

missing, my hands can't hold dream engines.
Curled in a ball in a clean lab unable

to bear being uncared for, a blue ruin,
no longer nasturtium, "cured" by "care."

Queen Quarantine

Why did they get more money for a two-
week flu than those who've been unable to

work since 1972 & those who
were born in bodyminds that can't tell time?

Boo-hoo, a year inside, try prison or
the hospital or five decades in my

life. But I've always been a trendsetter,
unemployed since 2007, self-isolating

from the age of eleven, none of this
is new for me. I haven't had company

since 2018 (Kirby, poetry's
good fairy). I am queen of unneeded,

so what quarantine? Some of us already
lived this way, locked-in, unloved & lonely.

Unidentifiable Lonely One

There's no apocalypse if I can get
a hand-delivered cup of sticky jizz

from a Cinnabon outlet. I am not
a victim or survivor of the system,

not a monster or a martyr or a
parent or a partner, keep undoing

opinions of what you oughta, not a
patient (but a poet?), not sister or

daughter or son or brother sun or some
kind of other unidentifiable

lonely one, not only body, not only mind,
do I know for sure I'll die? Everything

dies. "We take our lives so seriously"
said the cosmocrator to the indigo hind.

The Prime Directive

Hercules, Osiris, Jesus, the Fonz
on a surfboard, "No, it's Cheesus."

The Green Lantern, Neo in the Matrix,
there is no spoon. You are the Chosen One

& so are you. "There are always
other Skywalkers," says a Force ghost from

a hidden forest moon. This is your
letter from Hogwarts, we wizards have work

to do. Call off turf wars, unforge broadswords,
the Just Us League depends on you. Scarlet

witches & dark phoenixes, unleash. Doctor
X's little fixes are no worthy

nemesis. You are your own eternal
rebel alliance & apocalypse.

"To All the Boys, Cheerio"

I cancelled my subscription to the world
to dig my own diamond-minded playground

in Arcadia, drink absinthe from my own *kapala,*
play murderball with the Fell in absentia.

Bye-bye binary &
bananas, the singularity is

a Sham-wow, is it terribly bad man
ners to ask for a cannery on Death

Row? Who put the canary in the Fairy
Soap? Keep the washing up out of the post

al worker used to knock thrice. They knew my
name, that I am slow, they were nice. Where does

time go when it's not on ice? Her Highness
declines to comment on the empire's brides.

The Infernal Starshine of the Dauntless Mind

Blue rose in a glass cloche, old fool, the bell
jar's half-closed & cracked up. Pox flows as all

must to the boulevard. Johnny Panic
quit his day job to haunt the dive bars boarded

up when the world closed for repairs. No one
cares. Blanket the bluebells in burlap, April

colds in for the killsnap, protects pockets
with quick jabs, blood clots & loss spilled

on sweatshop rugs. We mine the detritus
of lost civilizations & stuff their leftovers

into our engines, iron: dragon blood,
mountains: tree stumps. Foxglove,

goldfinch, feldspar, are a part of this old
bitch's junkyard of janky bones.

Make Room, Bodymind Moon

March makes windows matter of fact. Go in
ward, be the fool. You are so prettiful,

like a tattered prayer flag. Gratitude can
call the bison back, undo the lie of lack.

Thank actual larches, literal lilac,
factual haskap. Gather moss with me.

I mean, stay at home & dig in. We can't
go back. If hate doesn't live here, where can

it go? If we throw it away it will
grow. Make room, make room, bodymind moon, none

need be touched to be part of. Welcome home.
In whatever state you are (undressed, un

sane, fucked up, in pain), this is home. This is
everyone's home & we are beloved.

Thank you Saint Joey,

for the medicine. Love gives four garbage
bags of weed to a relative stranger.

Love sends you a robot vacuum cleaner
wrapped in Tibetan paper. Love stitches

you a Babel fish & a sunset shawl.
Love drives their brother to chemo, gives up

weekends to demo drywall. Love doesn't
make you launch a book or suffer through the

weight of crowds. Love lets you cancel plans, turns
down the volume when the world gets too loud.

Love cooks dinner even when it's tired,
sacrifices to pay the bills on time.

Love puts the toothpaste in the tube, delivers
our food, takes away garbage when we're through.

Improbable Wildflowers

When the hyssop asked "What colour is your
Pain?" the river antlered. Hephaestus, I

no longer want to hide. Take off this armour,
open wide. It's just my own jealousy

of other bodyminds, ability
is wasted on the sane who spend their days

in shitty chairs in front of screens. They could
be climbing trees, floating downstream. I don't

trust the virus or the vaccine, the way
we ignore each other's needs & mask our own

pain. Can we cancel unkindness, shame on
improbable wildflowers, cast out hate?

I am the heart of the snake. My inner
peace is a community garden gate.

"All Shall Be Done,
   But It May Be Harder Than You Think."

Can we cancel unkindness, the lies that
divide us, ideas like yours & mine

are a virus, the iris makes the world
in its own imagine giving. Can we

cancel buying, the trial of sign-on-ins,
it's boring, the horror of form filling

& opinions can't cause harm. Gnosis,
why is it fine to let people die to

keep stores open? I keep hoping we out
grow war, set aside false pride, we die &

live & die & live & there are no sides.
The wardrobe door is in your mind, Narnia

the other side, we are god, a lion
with white swan wings, infinitely wide.

The Butcher's Table

Pan, play your pipes for Sappho & Hannibal,
into the dark call diabolical,

the Cannibal Priests lay the burial feast,
slabs of red meat that were the hungry

children of the Mother. There are horrors
in the garden falling ill. Follow Uncle

Nature under the barrow hill, lanterns
coronal lift shadows swallowing

angels eggshells hollow. Allow while blood
birds battle solitary bees by the

billions are scintillant Silmarillions
& the carillon call clarion

(Neptune never loved Orion), & other
untameable lions snowing from the sun.

Suns Moons Stars, Merely Bones

On the butcher's table slabs of old meat,
golden sardines, who gives a fuck what it means?

All shall perceive. Your souvenir is my
holy relic, an object that proves I left

this panic room at least for a day or
twenty-two steps to Sedlec's ossuary,

thirty-three rungs of vertebrae in a
Jacob's ladder. Does it matter? The great

celestial hierarchy of Scorpio:
suns moons stars, merely bones in a great

skeleton composed of all the substances
of the universe. We could do worse.

Draw nourishment by crown from our love
the sun. Leave monuments be. Make new ones.

"All Functions of Nature Reproduced in Miniature in the Body"

She becomes the sun & Her disciples
the twelve signs of the zodiac. Between

heaven & hell this middle garden,
the lobes of the cerebellum {Cain

& Abel}, am I its difference engine?
Spinal cord as flaming sword, nine

rattles in the serpent's tail sacred to
sacral & coccygeal. Here the pure

blue veil, Jupiter Janus, my eggeyes.
Be burning, a candle laid down. The winged

bone is a jewelled scarab carrying
the immortal spark. "The weaker, the more

sickly & the more nervous an individual
is, the better medium they will make."

Kapalabhati (Shining Skull Breath/Ego Eradicator)

Hunger anger uncle good girl, gun gun
gun gun gun, hunger anger uncle no

girl, gotta go gotta go gotta un
un un, hunger anger unclear ungirl,

ill love ill love ill love love, hunger &
ugly ugly gay girl, wanna go go

go gotta hungirl angirl uncle all
clear, gotta go gotta go gotta un

un un, no why, no why, why did they lie?
Gotta go, wanna go, want un un un

seen what girl, what love, what the fuck is love?
Hunger anger uncle god girl, un un

un hangry nuncle linger old girl, un
done undone undone undone undone done.

Do What Thou Wilt Shall Be The Whole of the Law

Beardtongue, bergamot, butterfly flower,
I took a walk in the old god's bower.

By "walk" I mean move by my own power
& when I say god I mean nature makes

us cower & we're cowards, still fearful
of each other as though every being

hasn't been our mother at one point or
another. Fear none, love all, plant many

flowers, make a garden from the grave of
the old man's tower. By "man" I mean no one

in particular is in charge, let none
sleep separate apart. Be as thou art,

do what thou wilt, make peace with the sheep,
possums, spiders, cripples, those we call least.

Selected References

A Course in Miracles by Helen Schucman, Viking: The Foundation for Inner Peace, 1976.

Angel's Egg directed by Mamoru Oshii, Studio Deen,1985.

Are You Experienced by The Jimi Hendrix Experience, Polydor Records, 1967.

Comfortable with Uncertainty: 108 Teachings on Cultivating Fearlessness and Compassion by Pema Chödrön, Shambhala Publications Inc., 2008.

"Dance on Vaseline" from the album *Feelings* by David Byrne, Luaka Bop/Warner Bros. 1997.

Dark Shadows, Dan Curtis Productions, 1969-1971.

David Lynch's daily weather report, *David Lynch Theatre*, YouTube.com.

Hannibal Lecter is borrowed from the work of Thomas Harris.

How to Change Your Mind: What the New Science of Psychedelics Teaches Us About Consciousness, Dying, Addiction, Depression, and Transcendence by Michael Pollan, Penguin Press, 2018.

KyletheRooster at YouTube.com.

Lay Down (Candles in the Rain) by Melanie, Buddah Records, 1970.

Living Beautifully with Uncertainty and Change by Pema Chödrön, Shambhala Publications Inc., 2013.

So Red the Rose by Arcadia, Capitol Records, 1985.

Spring, Summer, Fall, Winter...and Spring directed by Kim Ki-duk, Cineclick Asia, Sony Picture Classics, 2003.

"The Butcher's Table" by Nathan Ballingrud, from *Wounds: Six Stories from the Border of Hell*, Saga Press, 2019.

A Coney Island of the Mind by Lawrence Ferlinghetti, New Directions, 1958.

The Empty Man directed by David Prior, 20th Century Studios, 2020.

The Occult Anatomy of Man by Manly P. Hall, originally published 1929, Muriwai Books, 2018.

The White Goddess by Robert Graves, Faber & Faber, 1999.

Wild Strawberries directed by Ingmar Bergman, AB Svensk Filmindustri, 1957.

About the Author

The disabled poem-making entity known as Roxanna Bennett gratefully resides on aboriginal land. They are the author of the award-winning collections *The Untranslatable I* (Gordon Hill Press, 2021) and *Unmeaningable* (Gordon Hill Press, 2019).